Believe You Can

FOR ANYONE WHO WANTS TO GET THINGS DONE

GETTING STARTED & FINISHING IT

SHA'MECA OLIVER

FOUNDER OF PNEUMA BREATHE MINISTRIES, INC. AND DAUGHTER TO DAUGHTER

Believe You Can (Getting Started and Finishing It)
Copyright 2017 Sha'Meca Wynn-Oliver
ISBN: 978-0-9991524-0-9

Scripture quotation noted, AMP are from the amplified, KJV from the King James Version, and in NLT from the New Living Translation source BibleGateway.com – copyright 2017. Used by permission.

Scripture quotation noted, NIV New International Version, NIV Copyright 1973, 1978, 1984, 2011 by Biblical, Ic. Used by permission. All rights reserved worldwide./BibleGateway.com – copyright 2017. Used by permission.

Scripture quotation noted in NLT are taken from the Holy Bible, New Living Translation, copyright 1996, 2004, 2007 by Tyndale House Foundation. Used by permission of Tyndale House publishers, Inc., Carol Stream, IL 60188. All Rights Reserved.

All rights reserved, including reproduction of this book. This publication may not be reproduced, stored in a retrieval system or transmitted any form or by any means, electronically, mechanical, photocopying, recording, or otherwise.

Cover Design & Layout by: Wesley W. Oliver,
DreamsAliveProduction.com
Author photo by: Wesley W. Oliver
Editor: LaDonna Obafemi-Mitchell/Sha'Meca Oliver

Believe You Can
Getting Started & Finishing It

DEDICATION

I dedicate this book to **My Mom, Annette Little-Wynn,** who instilled in me the importance of putting God first and loving myself. No matter the situation, she always believed that I could accomplish anything I put my mind to doing. Her unconditional love for others, taught me to love without barriers, forgive quickly and help others to grow. I am truly blessed and grateful to be raised with her wisdom, understanding and strength.

My Grandmother – Verline Avery

She always taught her grandchildren to "Accept, no wooden nickels" She always made sure she was available to listen and never sugar-coated the truth.

My Sister – Melinda Cobb

She's a go getter. Her life exemplifies the title of this book. She has never allowed her life challenges to stop her from going after her dreams. She's one of the strongest women I know and admire. She has impeccable faith. I'm grateful to have a sister like her.

My Husband – Wesley Oliver
I'm thankful to him for allowing me to share my story with others without reservation. I'm thankful for his blessings as I committed to long hours of isolated studying and writing, while he watched our children and carried the weight of a lot things that I love to do. I thank him for loving me beyond my flaws, praying for me and supporting my dreams, even when he does not understand it all. His covering is more than words can express.

My Children - XI'Sairity, SeLacious & Chayim
One of the hardest challenges for me, honesty, has been raising children. Though my love for you all runs deep, my patience does not always. Every day, I make sure that I seek God for guidance on how to love you more, cultivate your gifts and how to grow as your mother, so that God gets the glory out of me as one of your parents. My trust in Him is the reason I believe I can do all things and it is becuaue of His strength. When you are old enough to understand the message that is in this book, you will understand that there is absolutely nothing short of greatness that you can have and can achieve; nothing is too hard for God to do in your life. But, you must work hard and trust Him for the expected outcome. You must know that Jeremiah 29:11 is written just for you.

Thank You

IV

TABLE OF CONTENTS

Who is Sha'Meca?	1
The Mountain Experience (Prelude)	5
A Need for Change	9
Believing You Can	17
Activity 1	27
Getting Started	33
Activity 2	41
Finishing It	47
Prayer of Encouragement	59
Affirmations	61
Journal	73

Who Is Sha'Meca?

I am a child of God; a wife, mother, friend, speaker, mentor, minister and entrepreneur. I am a woman who believes in pouring back into others to help build the best person they can be; whether the matter is spiritual, physical, mental or financial. I share from my heart, my journey, from my hurt, mistakes, tests, trials, triumphs as a growing woman. Because of my testimonies, I encourage others by saying, "You can make it in your career and personal life!" I love giving tips, tools and providing vehicles so others can experience their expected outcome. I am a mid-west gal, now residing on the east-coast, reaching an extended community of those who want to go to a greater level in their life.

I am an Alumni of Chicago State University, where I received my Bachelor's degree in Business Management. I have a Master's Degree in Management/Public Administration from Argosy University. I have utilized my degree to work for several not-for-profit organizations in education and administration. However, my career life has never dominated my entrepreneurial mindset and passion to help others. Even while I worked for different companies, I have always created opportunities to positively impact those whom I had worked and came in contact with, because I believe in making the best impact in every moment.

In 2003, I requested from my supervisor to be laid off from my civil service state employment job. I was privileged to know that many people I worked with were not happy working for 25 years, at the same place, and had not really enjoyed their full life. They weren't happy with their careers. They were only working to have a retirement check. I did not want that to be me. I wanted to enjoy my youth, college life and experience a bigger world. I challenged myself to believe that if I let go of what seemed great, that God would give me greater. I was willing to trust God for the unknown. Many people told me not to quit and some thought it was courageous. Who would have known, from the decision I made in September of 2003, that it would be the continuation of amazing things happening, even though, I still had to endure tests and trials?

When I decided to let go of the old (job) and to move into the new (everything ahead), I did not know that I would give birth to experiences that would build me the way that it did. I performed abroad, learned who I was and am, worried, empowered, fought through depression, accepted my flaws and gained strengths; bought a home, got married, had children, founded two ministries, etc; the journey con tinues.

So, I wrote this book and anticipate more to come, so that you can know how to start, finish and WIN through whatever you might face. Ultimately, the goal is to always, in every area of your life focus on BUILDING THE BEST YOU!

Though I share from my experiences, how you can "Believe you can, Get Started, And Finish it", I want you to read every word in this book with the intention of applying the tools and wisdom provided to your own situation. As you read, allow a fire to spark on the inside of you that encourages you to begin a new chapter in your life. You deserve to have the VERY BEST in every area of your life!

The Mountain Experience

Doesn't the first perception of our problems seem just like the mountain on the front cover of this book? Gigantic? Impossible to conquer? And when problems arise, we initially accept defeat without even sorting out the possibilities of a victory. So, how can you solve something that you have never faced or have the resources to solve it?

Go back to the front cover of this book. Picture yourself as that individual standing on that mountain. Now look to the far right, to the other side of that mountain. How will you get to the other side? And more than likely, if you are reading this book, you have probably have never climbed or crossed a mountain. Therefore, you probably do not have the clothing, the equipment, or have the knowledge on how to get this task done. All you know is that, if you want to achieve this goal, you must find a way to use what you have to get what you want.

For every problem, there is a solution. I believe the biggest problem is the process. Thinking about the process is a quick calculation of fear, skills, abilities, courage, the time it will take, the unknown and sudden onset of defeat. Subconsciously, this type of mindset can cause a person to lose the battle before even trying to win it. Do you want to win? Remember, every problem has an answer. That means someone has already solved it and it can be done. You just have to find your "HOW?" Now, for the next 30 seconds, I want you to close your eyes, take slow, deep, breaths, see yourself in position, at the top of that mountain and began to see your HOW.

Once you complete this book, you will definitely understand what I am talking about. I encourage you to believe that you are a mountain climber. Every problem that seems bigger than you, overwhelming, challenging or impossible, you must face it head on and conquer it. There is an overwhelming joy that accompanies a victory.

Caution, Mountain-climbing (dealing with the problem) is not easy. There are inclines, declines, the unfamiliar, plateaus, terrains, climate changes and the will to endure (the process) that you will need for this journey to get to the other side (the solution). Everything you decide to do to accomplish your goal is on the other side of the equal sign. The Solution can only be solved, if you work the problem. (My mother is a mathematician, so no wonder I am breaking this down this way).

AFFIRMATIONS

I encourage you, not for one second, to believe you must handle, hold-on to or settle for anything that is making you feel unworthy, that degrades you, and that does not support, compliment or cultivate God's predestined plan for your life. Sometimes, we deal with things we do not really have a desire for because we feel we can handle it or we want to make others happy, even though it can cause us to be unhappy and stressed out. If you live out other people's dreams, you will never accomplish yours.

Keep imagining yourself as the person on the cover of this book. You have started your journey. You have experienced some victories. And, now you are in the middle of that remote area, in the midst of trees, water, grassland and the unknown; between where you began the goal and where you plan to finish. You become tired and feel as though you have done enough. Do not give up on your first hope. You will never be fulfilled there. Inhale, exhale and keep going.

At times, this mountain experience will feel lonely. But, you are the only one who can achieve your goals. You are the only one who could feel your pain and that why you have to achieve this plan; your destiny is waiting on you to fulfill its purpose.

BELIEVE YOU CAN

CHAPTER ONE

A NEED FOR CHANGE

The first step to getting anything you want in life is **STARTING**. But, where do you start?

I was 19 years old, away at college at Northern Illinois University, in Dekalb, IL, trying to finish up my sophomore year. I was in a relationship that wasn't going to be the best for my future. At the time, there were things about my boyfriend that I was not feeling any more. He wasn't a bad person. He loved me. We knew each other from high school. We had great conversations. He would do almost anything in his strength to make sure I was happy. He was family oriented and he was attractive. Sounds like a great fit, right? But, I wasn't happy. There were layers of great attributes he possessed on the outside, but inside of me, I didn't see that my future would be bright with him.

During the season before our relationship was on the verge of ending, I began to find out that the things that made me happy and excited about him, well, most of it was a lie. And, because I loved him, just as much as he loved me, made it harder for me to let go; but I knew I had to take a leap of faith.

Sometimes when you are in love with someone (or, really like doing something), it will cause you to want to keep making an investment in them, in hopes that something will change for the better. But, I found out that sometimes having faith to stay with someone in hopes that things will improve, is the same type of faith that is needed when you need to release yourself from a person; especially when it is necessary to let go. This is because, it will not only free you to be better and do better, but it frees them, also.

I remember pondering on how I should break up with him. There were moments I cried. There were moments I thought about if he would be able to handle the break up. My decision was not overnight. For months, I was questioning my questions. During my thought process of potentially, breaking-up with him, I was still spending time with him. We held great conversations over the phone, but the feelings in my gut was bubbling and signaling that it was time to declare, quits!

Though, our conversations were still interesting, those too, were full of past lies. He fabricated his life events to continue to sound like he was telling the truth. So, why didn't I break up with him sooner knowing that he was no longer

CHAPTER ONE

right for me?

1. **Because he was my habit.** Anytime anything is a habit (good or bad, whether you like it or not) you go back to it. Habits are repetitive acts. You feel you need it. You treat it like a tradition. It is like brushing your teeth (you do it every day or schedule it). It is your norm. Your body craves it for energy. It's on your mind and your mind continuously thinks about whatever dominates it. Your feelings are attached to habits, because they gravitate to the things that drive them emotionally.

The Bible states in Proverbs 23:7, *"For as he thinketh in his heart, so is he…* (KJV) Therefore, as you think or do something over and over, it becomes a habit of thought or behavior; and that is who you become. However, habits can be broken.

2. **I loved him.** From a child, observing adults in my family, it was embedded in my subconscious that when you love someone, you do whatever you can for them; you do not leave, you put everything you have into the relationship, even if it starts to drain you. Well, at least that was the subliminal portrait that was painted for me. I watched women in my family fight for a type of happiness, they probably would never obtain.

3. **I was afraid of the unknown.** Fear can cripple any-

one. It can cause a person to be afraid of the unknown (not knowing if the expected outcome will actually work). Sometimes, it tricks you into believing that the worst can happen even with a good scenario. But, you will never know the outcome, if you never challenge the thing that is causing you to feel apprehensive.

I realized that if I wanted to be happy, if I wanted to know if I would have a better future without him, and if I could feel free without feeling like I am being selfish, inconsiderate or a terrible person, then I would have to end the relationship. I thought about staying friends with him, if that was at all possible. But, I knew that I had to take this step for myself. I needed to know if I could have better. I was hesitant, because trusting the unknown, did not provide comfort or guarantee a sure outcome. However, I needed to know if I could have better. Therefore, I was willing to risk it all to have what I deserved.

If you are reading this, that means you are a person, in a place, ready to get started on something new in your life or career; whether it is physically, spiritually, mentally, emotionally or financially. And, you want to experience and build a better you. You might be at a place of feeling tired of constantly holding on to unhealthy relationships or people. You might be tired of struggling with a poor mindset. You are probably ready to live healthier, ready to relocate, start a business or make a career change within or

CHAPTER ONE

outside of your current company. Or, if you are in college, you might be contemplating on changing to a major that fits you. You might even find yourself struggling with the thoughts of pleasing people, when all you really want to do is please yourself. Whatever your scenario might be, there is a solution for your circumstance.

What's Your Scenario?

The Need For Change, in order to Believe You Can starts with being honest with your authentic self. You must address all of the things that made you Believe You Can't.)

Below, you can write, short and honest notes about yourself and your situation; ie: What is it that you have to get started on in your life (goals)? What are your weaknesses? What are your shortcomings? What do you feel has been holding you back from moving forward? Is there anyone or anything hindering your growth?

CHAPTER ONE

Notes To Self:

"Trust God and believe that He will provide everything you need for your journey ahead!"

CHAPTER TWO

BELIEVING YOU CAN

When making a decision in life to do something better, for the purpose of **BUILDING THE BEST YOU**, one of the toughest battles to push pass, is believing you can, especially, when so many things from your past experiences have told you that you cannot attain the very best.

Our life experiences have a way of either motivating us to do better and live better, or they have a way of stripping us from believing we can attain greater. At times, our past experience makes us feel guilty if we dare to desire greatness. Sometimes, our lack to desire greater for ourselves stems from the things people have done to us. The lack of proper investment, has in some way, shape form or fashion, impacted our feelings and emotions. Believe it or not, those things have affected our character and our behavior. Feelings and emotions affect how we perceive ourselves, how we interact with others and they have our temperament. And, a lot of times, we live out the person we truly do not want to be. And, more than likely, it is because of the main three reasons I addressed in Chapter One that made me question if I should let go of an unhealthy relationship and that's dealing with the areas of:

1. How I love (Why I do what I do)

2. Habit (What I'm used to doing)

3. Fear (What I'm afraid of doing)

Maybe you want to pursue a new position but, you do not have the credentials. However, you do have the experience and the drive. Maybe you want to travel and teach abroad, but do not have the finances or connections. Maybe you want to be married, but you have witnessed so many failed marriages, which caused you to be afraid of being loved. Maybe you want to go to another level for yourself to feel beautiful again (or, for the first time), but because you have been talked about, misused or abused, it played a contributing role as to why you don't feel you deserve better. The discouragement you feel contributes to the things you have experienced while journeying through life. Instead of the experiences building you to be better, they picked at your self-esteem, chiseled your faith and made you feel unworthy. I want you to get your worth back!

To believe you can, to understand you are worthy of living, obtaining and being your best, does not began with your

CHAPTER TWO

feelings or emotions. Feelings and emotions are unstable. They change at any giving moment until you learn how to train and manage them. One minute you can want ice cream and the next minute you want pizza. So, do not allow your feelings and emotions become your driving factor, because they have the tendency to have you on an emotional rollercoaster. Know your truth and stand firm on it!

Believing you can and obtaining an expected outcome begins with dealing with the truth of your past. You must acknowledge whatever has caused discomfort. Then, begin thinking about the best outcomes as it pertains to the things you desire to obtain. The Bible says, "As a man thinketh in his heart,, so is he…" (Proverbs 23:7-KJV) Therefore, as you continuously began to train your thought patterns of wanting the best, you start working towards getting the best and becoming the best inside out. This process, allows the mind to cancel out all thoughts that said you could never accomplish something. Therefore, this new way of thinking will cause you to think on the things that say you can achieve an expected outcome.

The Bible also states, *"…Fix your thoughts on what is true, and honorable, and right, and pure, and lovely, and admirable. Think about things that are excellent and worthy of praise… Then the God of peace will be with you."* (Philippians 4:8 NLT) It is power in what you think. What you think has the power to influence what you do. And, thinking positively causes you to experience peace.

I believe that God wants you to experience the best of life; which is not all materialistic. I believe the best of life deals with the joy you can experience on the inside of you that must be evident on the outside of you in your daily living. I have said many times, that it is not enough for a person to have outer success (career, money, house, car) and be inwardly broken (depressed, suppressed, bitter, unhappy). You can have success both inside and out!

Jeremiah 29:11 states, *"For I know the plans I have for you," declares the Lord, "plans to prosper you not to harm you, plans to give you hope and a future."* (NIV) That means God has an expected outcome of increase and greatness for your life. Since, God has a plan for you to do great things. It is important for you to also have an aligned expectation.

It is time to have an expectation, whether you are dealing with people or some other factors, you are accountable for your own happiness and success. You have to choose to be happy and healthy. And, though people might be a contributing factor to why you feel like you do, no one has the power to keep you down. You have the ability to stand up anytime you are knocked off your feet.

In addition, the enemy (satan, lucifer, adversary, devil) does

CHAPTER TWO

not care who he attacks.

"Stay alert! Watch out for your great enemy, the devil. He prowls around like a roaring lion, looking for someone to devour." (1 Peter 5:8)

However, you do not have to be his victim. Your dreams, desires, happiness, joy and God's best for your life is not for the enemy to have; no matter how big, small or insignificant it might seem. Everything good, pertaining to your life, whether it is relationships, career, mental capacity, physical health and financial; God desires those things for you. He wants you to be blessed in every area of your life. Remember, even though, you have to let go of some things or sometimes detach yourself from someone, the need for separation can still be God's best for both of you. Therefore, don't feel guilty. It might be just that time to say good-bye to someone or something that has been hindering your growth.

One of the valuable lessons that I learned is that God does not want no one and nothing to take His place or come before Him.

"Do not make any gods to be alongside me; do not make for yourselves gods of silver or gods of gold." (Exodus 20:23)

Sometimes, it is easy to put so much of our attention on

completing things and pleasing people, that they become more of a priority than God. When we make people and things our primary focus, these people and things actually become gods in our life. And, anything that becomes our "god" is what we serve. What have you been letting dominate your mind and your life? What and who have you been serving? Once you figure this out, you must make a conscious decision that will start to focus your attention of what pleases God and not man.

> "Therefore, there is now no condemnation for those who are in Christ Jesus" (Romans 8:1)

Let Go of The Guilt!

It is easy to allow guilt to settle in to our minds; especially when we have a heart that desires to make things better in its current state. I want to encourage you to let go of the guilt syndrome, because it causes you to beat yourself up and it consumes you with thoughts that has the potential to persuade you from living your best life. Release yourself as quickly as you can from feeling like you owe someone or owe yourself something to stay in order to help, especially, when you know you need better.

Do not allow guilt to consume you. Know and trust that you are making a change to obtain God's best for your life. Do not feel as though if you hold on and continue to give chance after chance that you can, somehow, change the situation or that person. Let God be God! Let God be God for you, and allow God to be God for them! Let God workout any situation that you are facing? Trust God and believe that He will provide everything you need for your journey ahead!

Operate in Faith!

"Now faith is the substance of things hoped for, the evidence of things not seen." – Hebrews 11:1 (NKJV)

Through experience, I found out to stay doing something that does not provide growth or help build a better you, causes more damage to our health physically and spiritually than a person can imagine.

… The young man that I was dating at the time, I felt he needed me. See, I helped him build up his confidence. I knew most of his struggles. I was there to help him mend his relationship with his mom before she went home to glory. I was already welcomed in his family. I was one of the only persons that could drive his granddad's car (I barely had a license or knew how to drive). I went to almost all of his family functions. He knew my entire family. My family liked him. He knew my struggles, and so on. I mean, the more I contemplated about what I should do about this relationship, the more I made myself feel guilty for wanting to move forward. I really was

beating myself up. And, to think, I was at the very young age of 19.

Wow, 19 years old!

I was in the process of making decisions that would lay a strong foundation for my life:

1. Choosing Faith over Fear
2. Stepping Outside My Comfort Zone
3. To Be a God Pleaser & Not a People Pleaser
4. Trusting God's Plan for My Life
5. Not Letting my Emotions Dominate What I Needed

Your decision today can lay a strong foundation for tomorrow and for generations to follow.

Side note: One of the reasons I am excited about writing this book, is because it is not just for a particular type of person or age group. It is not for the intentions to puff up or to give someone a temporary excitement. But, it is for you (a person who can really have success inside and out)!

My desire is for you to know that you can do what feels impossible, if you begin to believe you can. But, also to realize that our thought processes and how we handle situations in life does affect us. Hurt, the lack of love and support have challenges. Those challenges does not dis-

criminate whose life it invades. However, what you decide to do about it has to be your focus.

In life there is always a decision making process. When it comes to making a decision, in order to believe you can, your age does not matter; neither does your financial or social status. What does matter is being able to push pass the negative and deeply-rooted things that have influenced your behaviors/struggles/worth/perception of yourself and do not let it define the person you are destined to become. You're past is not permanent, the future is always ahead!

Time To Grow!

Embracing and accepting the challenge for the need to grow at 19 years, prepared me to be aware of many barriers that can hinder growth in not just me, but anyone. It allowed me to trust my own instincts and always position myself to reach towards obtaining the best; which caused me to know who I am, to Whom I belonged and who I am capable of becoming. Trials and tribulations come to us all, but they come to make us better! Do not allow your past to dictate your future, nor let it stop you from having an exceptional one!

You have to GROW-UP to Go-UP!

"When I was a child, I spake as a child, I understood as a child, I

thought as a child: but when I became a man, I put away childish things." – 1 Corinthians 13:11

Like a man who once was a child, you are growing from one stage in your life to another. In order for you to get better results, you must think on a more mature level. The things that you used to do and how you used to think has to change. It is time to let go of your old way of doing things and developing a new way of getting the results you desire.

It is time for you to be on the road towards making a decision. No matter the trial, tribulation or situation, it is time to go to a greater level. Believing You Can, is the first way you are going to begin to experience change.

CHAPTER TWO

Activity 1

In the space below, write down everything you want to happen for you in your life. Write down the places you want to go. Write down the dreams you want to accomplish. Write down the things you want to experience. Write down why you need to do things for you. Write down your fears. Write down your areas of confidence. Write down the great things you do for people. After you look at these things and you might read your lists over and over. All of these things are a part of making decisions for the next level. When you can be authentic and honest with your own-self, you can be okay with loving your strengths, but you must also be okay with owning your weaknesses:

BELIEVE YOU CAN

Activity 1 Cont...

CHAPTER TWO

This activity is designed to do several things:

1. Help you goal set

2. Identify purpose

3. Bring your skeletons to the forefront

4. Cause you to encourage yourself

5. Stir up your faith

6. Activate Change

This activity will help you realize why you deserve to have the best; therefore, it should encourage you to not be afraid to get the success you deserve.

BELIEVE YOU CAN

Note to Self:

CHAPTER TWO

"...being able to push pass the negative and deeply-rooted things that have influenced your behaviors/struggles/worth/perception of yourself and do not let it define the person you are destined to become."

BELIEVE YOU CAN

CHAPTER THREE

GETTING STARTED

Are You Ready?
Get set?
Go!

At this point your mind should be made up. You should know what you want, rather, know what you need. There is a difference between a want and a need. A "Want" is a personal desire. It is when you feel you must have something because it will make you happier. It is a temporary satisfaction. It has nothing to do with advancing you to the next level. A "Need" can be a personal desire, too. However, the desire to have it is not based off of self-fulfillment. A need constitutes something that is necessary to obtain, because it is essential for your growth and the betterment of your situation. You should be able to see it building you! And, you should see yourself moving towards the end goal. However, accomplishing your goal is more than just thinking it and writing it down. It is the opportunity to move from paper and pen to living out what you wrote. Are you ready to start building the best you!?

What are your wants?

What are your needs?

CHAPTER THREE

At this point you must make a decision to focus on your needs, rather than your wants. Because, you should not want a temporary fix but permanent results.

> *"And the Lord answered me, and said, write the vision, and make it plain upon tables, that he may run that readeth it."*
> *(KJV)*

It is time to **WRITE** AND **RUN**!

The best way to accomplish any goal in life is to start! You cannot get the job done, if you do not start the process.

The Pre-Break Up

…I had to do this, but how? How was I going to tell someone who loved me, whom I loved, that we could no longer continue as a couple? What if I crush his heart (even though my heart was crushed)? I sat in my room and my heart leaned towards a place that desired peace.

(I usually pray about everything. At this point, I do not remember praying about my final decision. I believe that I prayed and talked with God so much that He was waiting on me to have faith in the decision that I needed to make. I do believe that God will give us thoughts that line up with His thoughts. Therefore, we have access to wisdom that we could not have out of our own strength.) I believe that God gave me a simplistic way of making one of the biggest decisions for my life, at the time.

Examples of Questions to ask yourself when making your decision for change:

1. What is my need for change?

i.e. My need for change is to have greater physical health.

2. What is it that I need to change in order to accomplish my goals?

i.e. I need to change how I think about my health, my eating habits and start exercising.

3. Why do I need to change?

i.e. Not only do I want to feel good physically, I want to look good to myself. I believe good health equals longevity.

4. How will I accomplish it?

i.e. I am going to commit to eliminating whatever has been hindering my progression.

CHAPTER THREE

Activity 2

The bible teaches that the importance of writing the vision down and making it plain is so that when it is read, the person who reads it will "Run". (Habakkuk 2:2) When you write down the things that you desire, you have clarity and a tangible reminder of the things you need to accomplish. Therefore, you can have a reference of what you need to do, accomplish it and be motivated and encouraged to do it! You must see it; believe it and do it.

Start Accomplishing The Plan

... It was time to start the process of truth to accomplish my purpose and start my journey to reach my expected outcome.

And, I did and so can you:

1. I got a plain sheet of paper

2. I got a pen

3. I drew a line down the middle of the paper

4. On the left side of the line I wrote the word "likes" and underlined it and on the right side of the line, I titled it "dislikes" and underlined it

5. At the top of the paper write the name of the person or thing you are referring to

6. Under the likes column, write down everything you like about the person or the thing and number it

7. Under the dislike column, write down everything you dislike about the person or thing and number it

Example:

Name of Person/Place/Thing:_____

LIKES	DISLIKES
1.	1.
2.	2.
3.	4.
5.	5.
6.	6.
7.	7.
8.	8.
9.	9.
10.	10.

I knew I had to write this down, because I was thinking too much. And the more I thought about ending the relationship, the more I doubted myself. Continuously having conversations with him, did not work. All it did was give

CHAPTER THREE

me excuses to stay in something that was not meant for me. And, it has been said before by many people throughout my life, if you are doing the same thing, getting the same poor results, it is called, "insanity." I needed peace and I needed sanity.

Write the Vision make it plain...

...There it was, written down and it was like each dislike was staring me in my face and had its own heartbeat. I was finally faced with my truth. I started to make myself believe that all of the dislikes that I wrote down was out of selfishness and maybe it was something I deserved. However, I knew that was not true. Though I was feeling a particular way, I knew he did not deserve to have anyone who was not feeling him anymore, because I would not be able to give him the relationship that he needed to become his best.

Releasing yourself from someone has benefits for them, too.

My dislikes outweighed my likes. My dislikes continued on the back of my paper. It was not because he was a horrible person. But, I asked myself question that pertained to my perception of how our future would look like if we were to continue to make efforts to make the relationship work. I pondered, "How would we live? Where would we reside? Do our visions collide? Could he build me?"
Wait! You are probably thinking, that I was thinking too

much into this relationship. But, when a person who you have been dating from high school to college, who has the possibility of becoming your husband, and cannot stop lying about his income, education, dates and events that happened in his life, so that he can feel worthy enough to have you, it becomes unhealthy. I would not have been able to trust him or, really get to know the real him. Therefore, it was better for him to start over new with someone that he could be authentic with for years to come. Not only did I need a do-over, he needed one, too. Remember, whatever cannot build you has the potential to break you or leave you stagnant.

I remember, throughout the years of dating him, one of his siblings would always tell me that he was lying, but she joked so much about life events, that I did not believe her. (Do we, at times, get that hint/inclination about things we should stop doing before we get too deeply involved?) I learned that it is very important to pay attention to signs and have discernment.

"A wise man will hear, and will increase learning; and a man of understanding shall attain unto wise counsels..." (Proverbs 1:5)

Though my dislikes outweighed my likes, I still had to make the decision to let go of the relationship. Getting started is not just about coming to grips with what you need to do. It is about knowing what you need to do, start the race, and

CHAPTER THREE

cross the finish line. Any time you are in position to run a race, you have to keep running.

I still had work to do.

Activity 2

Now, it is your turn. It is your opportunity to reference your concern/issue and write down every like and dislike and then make a conscious decision to let go or hold on.

#1 Name of Person/Place/Thing:_____

LIKES	DISLIKES
1.	1.
2.	2.
3.	4.
5.	5.
6.	6.
7.	7.
8.	8.
9.	9.
10.	10.
11.	11.
12.	13.
14.	14.
15.	15.
16.	16.
17.	17.
18.	18.
19.	19.
20.	20.

Your list might exceed this list. Whatever the case, you must make a decision to stay in your current situation or move beyond it.

What is your decision? _____

CHAPTER THREE

Here's your opportunity to work out another issue.

#2 Name of Person/Place/Thing:_____

LIKES	DISLIKES
1.	1.
2.	2.
3.	4.
5.	5.
6.	6.
7.	7.
8.	8.
9.	9.
10.	10.
11.	11.
12.	13.
14.	14.
15.	15.
16.	16.
17.	17.
18.	18.
19.	19.
20.	20.

What is your decision? _____

#3 Name of Person/Place/Thing:_____

LIKES	DISLIKES
1.	1.
2.	2.
3.	4.
5.	5.
6.	6.
7.	7.
8.	8.
9.	9.
10.	10.
11.	11.
12.	13.
14.	14.
15.	15.
16.	16.
17.	17.
18.	18.
19.	19.
20.	20.

What is your decision? _____

CHAPTER THREE

Notes to Self:

"...knowing what you need to do, start the race, and cross the finish line."

CHAPTER FOUR

FINISHING IT

Consistency is key.

If you say you are going to get in shape, you have to work out until you lose the weight, then keep up with the regiment to maintain the results. If you say you are going to be financially stable, you have to learn to save or invest wisely and keep doing it until you get the expected outcome. If you say you are going to have a better mindset, you have to train your thoughts to think better, stop complaining and speak positive. If you say you are going to do anything, you have to get started, stick with it and make things happen.

I know that I have been sharing with you my relationship woes as a young adult, but the same principle works with any situation. Even though I was a young, this process was vital for my success. And, yours, too!

And, it continues:

...So, in the middle of the day, I was driving in the first car I ever bought (a Ford Focus) and truly wanted, other than an Astro van that me and my friend both wanted (We used to shout, "bingo", every time we saw an Astro Van); and I was at a drive through of one of my go-to-fast-food restaurants getting me a sandwich and a frozen beverage from the dollar menu. I called him. At first, I was nervous, but ready. I was respectful, as always. I greeted him with hello and asked him how he was he doing. I became calm and confident. I continued the conversation by telling him that I wanted to talk about us. I explained that I did not want to continue the relationship and gave all my reasons why.

Of course, he did not want to break up. He wanted us to start over. I could not back out of my decision. I had to hold my ground and trust that my decision was best for me. At this point, the break-up was not hard for me, because I was prepared.

Important Things to Remember:

1. Be Prepared

2. Acknowledge, Know & Own the Issue

3. Decide what you're going to do

4. Know why you have to make the change

CHAPTER FOUR

5. Make a decision

6. Start the decision process

7. And, Do it

... We Broke Up!

But wait, it was not finished. Remember, Consistency is key. Even though I achieved the break-up part, I had to make sure I did not go back to the very thing that I decided was not promising for me.

A lot of times when we initially set a goal, we are on fire, pumped up and we excitingly tell almost everyone that will listen. Then after we start seeing results, we slowly slip back into our old ways because we have failed to break the habits.

Yes, my decision making process to break off the relationship was difficult at first because I did things out of habit in our relationship. I was used to picking up the phone every time he called. I was used to spending time. I was used to him being an answer to things I wanted, whether it was a ride or conversation. However, habits can be broken.

What habits do you need to break?

The Bible states in 1 Timothy 4:7-8 to:

> "...*train yourself to be godly. "Physical training is good, but training for godliness is much better, promising benefits in this life and in the life to come."*

The key word is train:

Any time you want to break a habit, you have to train yourself not to do it. Any time you want to do something you have to train yourself to do it.

This scripture is powerful! I apply it to almost everything I do and teach, because, it infers the importance of not only being consistent in life, but it implies living life with purpose. And, it implies living life on purpose. It encourages discipline and obedience. It also teaches the importance of keeping God as your main objective for a promised outcome, therefore, the things that you want to have will not be a temporary fulfillment, but something to sustain permanently.

Also, 1 Timothy 4:7-8 starts off encouraging the reader to spend time and energy training yourself. When you train yourself in anything, you do it over and over until it becomes your norm.

Being that I am a dancer, I can relate to this all so well. Whenever I was in practice and could not get the hang of a dance move, I would have to practice it over and over until my body would remember it. It is called, muscle memory. Until you get what you want deep down on the inside of you, do not stop. Having a successful mind, career, relationship, and life is possible.

Now let us address more truth:

Everybody will not understand your "Why." They will not always understand your reason for desiring change in your life. Everyone will not be your cheerleader and sometimes, those who have cheered for you in the past, might not cheer for you in your present situation. At times you must have tough skin and have to cry alone. You might experience trials and errors, but if you want to experience the success you have talked about, you have to work on it & be consistent and get it done. You do not want to go back to the things that hinder your success. You must BELIEVE YOU CAN!

Important Note:

I did not do this on my own. I had to trust that if I let go, God's best was still available for my life. I had to trust and believe that God's plan for my life was filled with prosperity, purpose and a plan.

(Jeremiah 29:11) was truth for me:

"For I know the plans I have for you," says the Lord. "They are plans for good and not for disaster, to give you a future and a hope."

...After the break up, my ex-boyfriend and I kept in contact. We sporadically, talked on the phone, laughed and shared family and relationship updates. As for me, there were no feelings of wanting to reconnect as a couple. He met someone else, they had two children together and eventually, he married someone else. As for me, I married an awesome man of God, we have three beautiful children, a great ministry and a whole lot of encouragement to share.

I finished the goal!

Finishing what you start is a great feeling. And, experiencing the expected outcome is even greater! Whether your dream/goal is to write a book, journey across the world, apply for a new position, attend school, build the best you; you will never know that you can actually achieve it, if you never get started.

But, Wait!

Now, let's go back to the prelude of this book. Remember this:

"Understand that the top of that mountain is only your starting

CHAPTER FOUR

point. Getting to the other side is when you can say you have made it. But, getting back to ground level is when you can say you have finished it?"

Do you get it, now?

You will know when you have finished your goal *when know how to live after the victory.* It is when you are not afraid to fall in love again and trust someone with your heart to fulfill God's predestined purpose in your life. You have finished, when you are able to move forward in your goals and not allow others to dictate who you are and what you should be doing. It is when decide to live out your desires because you understand your purpose without feeling condemned. You are finished when you know what it took to get you to where you are, and when do not allow anything to convince you to relive, revisit and rekindle what you have already allowed to cease. YOU MUST KNOW HOW TO LIVE AFTER THE VICTORY!

Remember this:

"When you go to war against your enemies and see horses and chariots and an army greater than yours, do not be afraid of them, because the LORD your God, who brought you up out of Egypt, will be with you. When you are about to go into battle, the priest shall come forward and address the army. He shall say: "Hear, Israel: Today you are going into battle against your

enemies. *Do not be fainthearted or afraid; do not panic or be terrified by them. For the LORD your God is the one who goes with you to fight for you against your enemies to give you victory."* (Deuteronomy 20:1-4)

God is with you. Don't Worry.

Just look to the Hills...

*"I will lift up mine eyes unto the hills, from whence cometh my help.
My help cometh from the Lord, which made heaven and earth.
He will not suffer thy foot to be moved: he that keepeth thee will not slumber.
Behold, he that keepeth Israel shall neither slumber nor sleep.
The Lord is thy keeper: the Lord is thy shade upon thy right hand.
The sun shall not smite thee by day, nor the moon by night.
The Lord shall preserve thee from all evil: he shall preserve thy soul.
The Lord shall preserve thy going out and thy coming in from this time forth, and even for evermore." (Psalm 121)*

CHAPTER FOUR

Notes To Self:

BELIEVE YOU CAN

"If you say you are going to do anything, you have to get started, stick with it and make things happen."

CHAPTER FOUR

BELIEVE YOU CAN

A PRAYER FOR YOU

My prayer is that you are ready to "Believe You Can" accomplish anything you put your mind to and become who God has predestined you to be; no matter your situation. I pray that you begin to get started on that great vision that you see for your future and complete the tasks that is ahead of you; to experience an expected outcome. I pray that you hear God in the midst of your trial and trust Him. And, that you will have the courage to say no to anything that is not God's best for you, so that you can be successful inside and out.

Lord, I thank you for the person who has invested their time and attention to reading this book. I pray that they would have strength, courage and trust in You to let go of anything that would hinder his/her growth and the purpose that You have predestined for them. I pray that they would trust You with their future and everyone and anything in it. And, though they might experience trials, those trials will not hinder their growth, but make them wiser and stronger.

What is it that you want God to do for you? (write your prayer below):

Dear God:

Your Child,

7 DAYS OF AFFIRMATIONS

There is Power In What You Decree!

Job 22:28 (KJV)

> *"Thou shalt also decree a thing, and it shall be established unto thee: and the light shall shine upon thy ways."*

You have the authority to speak greatness over your entire life and everything that you are a part of and anything that is a part of you!

The next seven pages are seven affirmations that you can use to decree and declare over your life, daily. When you decree a thing, it has the power to achieve what you speak (speak positively). It has the power to override any negative thoughts or influences that may have made you think you can't, but now you know that you can!

BELIEVE YOU CAN

Day 1

I will seek God First and will live for Him. My ways please the Lord

(Proverbs 16:7)

AFFIRMATIONS

Day 2

I can complete all of my goals.
(Philippians 4:13)

Day 3

I am a great person inside and out; others love that about me.

(Philippians 4:5)

AFFIRMATIONS

Day 4

Everything is working out for my good. I will not worry. I will trust God for the outcome.

(Hebrews 11:6)

Day 5

I can say no to the things that are no good for me. I am consistent and disciplined.

(Titus 2:12)

AFFIRMATIONS

Day 6

I will give grace and have mercy for others, no matter the situation.

(Isaiah 30:18)

Day 7

I will diligently work on building the best me.

(Isaiah 66)

AFFIRMATIONS

Notes to Self:

"For I know the thoughts that I think toward you, saith the Lord, thoughts of peace, and not of evil, to give you an expected end. Then shall ye call upon me, and ye shall go and pray unto me, and I will hearken unto you. And ye shall seek me, and find me, when ye shall search for me with all your heart."

Jeremiah 29:11-13

AFFIRMATIONS

You Can Achieve Great Things!

Believe You Can

BELIEVE YOU CAN

AFFIRMATIONS

Journal

BELIEVE YOU CAN

AFFIRMATIONS

BELIEVE YOU CAN

AFFIRMATIONS

BELIEVE YOU CAN

AFFIRMATIONS

BELIEVE YOU CAN

AFFIRMATIONS

BELIEVE YOU CAN

AFFIRMATIONS

BELIEVE YOU CAN

AFFIRMATIONS

BELIEVE YOU CAN

AFFIRMATIONS

BELIEVE YOU CAN

AFFIRMATIONS

BELIEVE YOU CAN

AFFIRMATIONS

BELIEVE YOU CAN

AFFIRMATIONS

BELIEVE YOU CAN

AFFIRMATIONS

BELIEVE YOU CAN

AFFIRMATIONS

BELIEVE YOU CAN

AFFIRMATIONS

BELIEVE YOU CAN

AFFIRMATIONS

www.ingramcontent.com/pod-product-compliance
Lightning Source LLC
LaVergne TN
LVHW051506070426
835507LV00022B/2949